ON A MISSION

Special Forces

ON A MISSION

Bomb Squad Technician

Border Security

Dogs on Patrol

FBI Agent

Fighter Pilot

Firefighter

Paramedic

Search and Rescue Team

Secret Service Agent

Special Forces

SWAT Team

Undercover Police Officer

ON A MISSION

Special Forces

By Matthew Marini

Mason Crest
450 Parkway Drive, Suite D
Broomall, PA 19008
www.masoncrest.com

Printed and bound in the United States of America.

Series ISBN: 978-1-4222-3391-7
Hardback ISBN: 978-1-4222-3401-3
EBook ISBN: 978-1-4222-8510-7

First printing
1 3 5 7 9 8 6 4 2

Produced by Shoreline Publishing Group LLC
Santa Barbara, California
Editorial Director: James Buckley Jr.
Designer: Bill Madrid   Production: Sandy Gordon
www.shorelinepublishing.com
Cover image: courtesy U.S. Navy.

Library of Congress Cataloging-in-Publication Data

Marini, Matthew, 1970-
        Special forces / by Matthew Marini.
        pages cm -- (On a mission!)
        Includes index.   Audience: Grades 7-8.
ISBN 978-1-4222-3401-3 (hardback) -- ISBN 978-1-4222-3391-7 (series) -- ISBN 978-1-4222-8510-7 (ebook)
 1. Special forces (Military science)--United States--Juvenile literature. 2. United States. Navy. SEALs--Juvenile literature.
 I. Title.
UA34.S64M367 2015
356'.160973--dc23
                                                            2015009752

Contents

Key Icons to Look For

Words to Understand: These words with their easy-to-understand definitions will increase the reader's understanding of the text, while building vocabulary skills.

Sidebars: This boxed material within the main text allows readers to build knowledge, gain insights, explore possibilities, and broaden their perspectives by weaving together additional information to provide realistic and holistic perspectives.

Research Projects: Readers are pointed toward areas of further inquiry connected to each chapter. Suggestions are provided for projects that encourage deeper research and analysis.

Text-Dependent Questions: These questions send the reader back to the text for more careful attention to the evidence presented here.

Series Glossary of Key Terms: This back-of-the-book glossary contains terminology used throughout this series. Words found here increase the reader's ability to read and comprehend higher-level books and articles in this field.

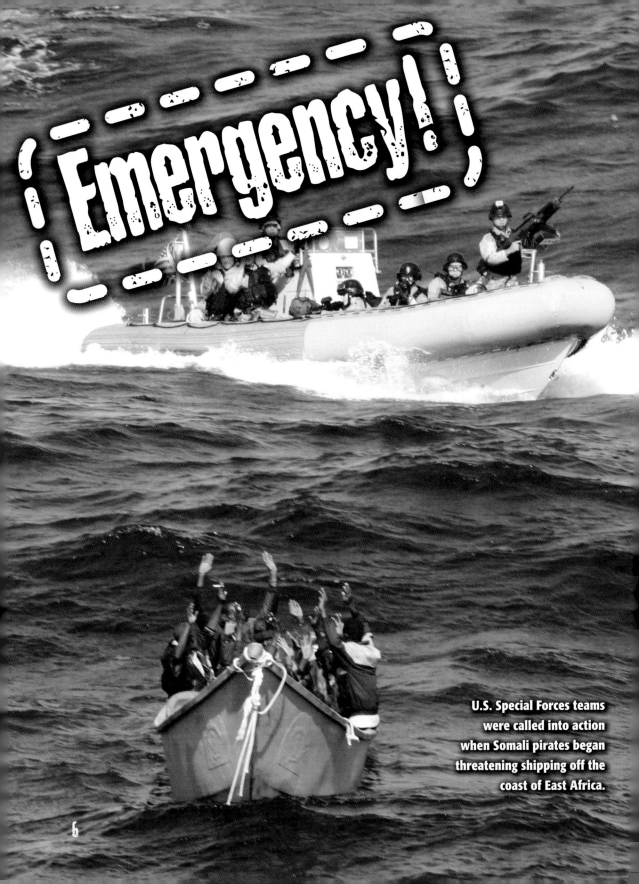

Emergency!

U.S. Special Forces teams were called into action when Somali pirates began threatening shipping off the coast of East Africa.

It had been more than two hundred years since a United States-flagged ship was hijacked by pirates. To most people, pirates were only real in Johnny Depp movies, or as Halloween costumes. In the Indian Ocean and the Persian Gulf region, though, pirates were becoming all too real.

The country of Somalia had a struggling economy, and its citizens were desperate. Some turned to criminal acts as a way of life. Armed with guns and rockets while patrolling the waters in small boats, Somali pirates had begun to make headlines. They hijacked commercial ships dozens of times and demanded large **ransoms** from other countries. When these payments arrived, some in excess of a million dollars, the pirates would allow the ships to sail away.

The United States government was very aware of the problems with pirates in the region. Thankfully, and intelligently, the pirates had steered clear of American vessels…until now.

The container ship *Maersk Alabama* was sailing off the coast of Somalia in 2009. The 500-foot (152-m) ship carried a 20-person crew

Words to Understand

AK-47s a type of assault rifle

mayday an international distress signal

ransoms money that is paid in order to free someone who has been captured or kidnapped and millions of dollars of food and humanitarian goods for the people of nearby Kenya. Roaring up to the ship in fast-attack boats, four Somali pirates boarded the vessel armed with **AK-47s**. After a battle with the crew, the pirates abandoned the ship by climbing into one of the motorized lifeboats with the *Maersk Alabama's* captain, Richard Phillips, as hostage.

Before being captured, Phillips sent out a **mayday** signal that was received by the USS *Bainbridge*, under the command of Commander Frank Castellano. The U.S. Navy destroyer had been in the area and, fortunately, had a Somali interpreter on board. Traveling at top speed, it took a day for the *Bainbridge* to reach the area where the hijacking had taken place.

When the *Bainbridge* arrived, it bombarded the hijacked ship with bright lights and loud sirens. In the confusion, Marines boarded the *Maersk Alabama* and freed the crew. However, Castellano soon realized that Captain Phillips was not on board. He had another rescue to arrange.

Castellano had excellent crew members aboard his destroyer. They could handle almost any mission. However, as he considered sneaking on to a motorized raft with a hostage guarded at gunpoint, he knew he needed help. He got on the radio and called in the Navy SEALs, one of the world's most elite military Special Forces.

The USS *Bainbridge* steamed rapidly into the conflict zone. The warship would soon be joined by the elite Navy SEALs.

Later, in the chapter "Mission Accomplished," read how SEALs came to the rescue. First, find out how the SEALs and other Special Forces came to be, and meet the brave men and women who volunteer for the challenge.

Chapter 1

With today's high-tech communications gear, a Special Forces soldier can go anywhere to complete his mission.

Mission Prep

Nations have had armies for thousands of years. Those military units defend the nation, fight in wars, rescue people, and carry out the orders of their leaders. Most parts of the military operate in the open, marching, flying, or riding to wherever they are ordered. Their missions are reported in the news and covered in history books. Some jobs done by the military, however, call for another kind of unit. They are known as Special Forces. Armies around the world call on small, elite units of highly trained soldiers to take on daring and important jobs. Often these are completed in great secrecy. Some of the most successful, and bravest, Special Forces soldiers will never be known except by one another.

Words to Understand

demolition destruction in war by means of explosives

deployed move (troops) into position for military action

earmark a characteristic or identifying feature

fatigues nickname for camouflage uniforms worn by armies

guerrilla warfare irregular military actions carried out by small forces

integral necessary to make a whole complete

maritime connected with the sea

Special Forces Ancestors

Prior to 1952, the U.S. military had groups that acted as Special Forces, though they were not called that yet. During World War II, branches of the military created hastily formed groups that carried out numerous vital missions. Among these groups were the Navy Underwater **Demolition** Teams (UDTs).

During World War II, the UDTs had a mission to attack Kwajalein in the South Pacific. A UDT was sent on a rubber boat to scout the island prior to the operation. However, a coral reef prevented the team from landing. The UDTs stripped off their **fatigues**, boots, life jackets, and metal helmets and, wearing just their boxers, swam to shore undetected. They were able to return with the necessary sketches to launch a successful attack. Naval

Combat Swimming became a vital task for UDTs and, later, Navy SEALs. World War II also saw the birth of the Army's Office of Strategic Services (OSS). That unit often worked out ahead of advancing divisions to conduct operations behind enemy lines and support the resistance groups.

At the conclusion of World War II in 1945, the UDTs disbanded. Later, military leaders saw the advantage of that kind of creative, brave, and quick-acting team. Other nations formed Special Forces units during and after World War II. Great Britain had the Commandos and the Special Air Service (SAS). The Soviet Union created Spetsnaz. Israel formed Shayetet 13. The SAS in particular became a model for Special Forces around the world.

When the Korean War began in 1950, the UDTs were quickly started up again. Larger Army units took the name Special Forces in the 1950s as well. They also earned their unofficial nickname, Green Berets, for their familiar headgear. These Special Forces were a land-based force of soldiers who took on missions behind enemy lines in the Vietnam War. Special Forces soldiers earned 17 Congressional Medals of Honor during that conflict.

Here Come the SEALs

In 1961, during a famous speech to Congress, President John F. Kennedy spoke of dreams such as landing a man on the Moon. In that same address, Kennedy also noted the need to strengthen the United States's military forces. Kennedy said he would **earmark** more than $100 million to help the military's Special Forces units.

The following year, in 1962, the United States Navy SEALs were established as part of the U.S. Special Operations Command. SEALs conduct small-unit, **maritime** military missions. Navy SEALs are trained to be at full strength in various environments (Sea, Air, and Land), from which they took the group's unique name. They have become one of the most famous and recognizable Special Forces.

Once the Navy SEALs were created, they were needed almost immediately to help combat the **guerrilla warfare** and night-water missions of the Vietnam War. Many of the first SEALs were members of the UDT units that had helped during the Korean War and other events during the 1950s. The men quickly were trained for various physical duties, such as hand-to-hand combat and high-altitude parachuting, or skills such as cracking a safe or learning other languages.

In 1963, the Central Intelligence Agency (CIA) began to use the SEALs for covert operations in Vietnam. Over time, the SEALs began to realize that when they had the opportunity to develop their own information prior to the attack, the operation had a higher success rate.

During their involvement in the Vietnam War from 1965 to 1972, 46 SEALs were killed. It is shocking to consider the death toll was not higher considering the SEALs often fought the war hand-to-hand with

SEAL teams went "upriver" in Vietnam, often working behind enemy lines to gather intelligence.

their opponents. The SEALs and other Special Forces proved to be the United States's most effective antiguerrilla branch during the war.

To this day, the SEALs and the other Special Forces branches are an **integral** part of the U.S. military. Some of their stories are told in the following pages.

Special Forces Today

In 1977, Army Colonel Charles Beckwith realized the Army needed a strike force to deal with the threat of terrorism that was beginning to envelop the world. Beckwith started Delta Force, based off his time working with the British Special Air Service earlier in the decade. Delta Force was designed to be similar to the SEALs, but with a greater emphasis on land warfare and tactics.

In 1983, America invaded the tiny Caribbean island of Grenada, in an effort to help American medical students get off the island during a war that was going on there. It was America's first combat in nearly a decade, and was the first time that the Delta Force, Army Rangers, and Navy SEALs were all put into action. Army Rangers parachuted onto the island to round up the students, guide them to the beach, and help them aboard Sea Knight helicopters to fly off the island. In all, 740 American citizens were evacuated, including 595 students. SEALs and Delta Force struck other parts of the island in what was an overwhelming success.

Walking down a wall? During a training exercise, this Army Ranger practices a unique way of reaching an objective.

During the early 1990s, Special Forces were a key part of the first Iraq War. As the leader of Operations Desert Shield and Desert Storm, General H. Norman Schwarzkopf said, "Special Forces were the eyes and ears on the ground." From there, Special Forces conducted missions in Haiti, Bosnia, Kosovo, and in other locales around the world. Of course, those are just the missions that made the news. With the secret nature of some Special Forces operations, it's likely there were other missions that we might never hear about.

After the terrorist attacks of September 11, 2001, the elite military units were **deployed** in Afghanistan and Pakistan as the United States searched for the Taliban. It was a Special Forces unit named SEAL Team Six that successfully tracked down and killed terrorist leader Osama Bin Laden in 2011.

Today, Special Forces are being used at record levels. In 2014 alone, U.S. Special Operations forces were deployed to 133 countries.

Joining Special Forces

To be part of a Special Forces unit, a person must already be enlisted in a branch of the military. Soldiers have to go through basic training before requesting permission to try out for the Special Forces. Before they even attend a training session, applicants are carefully screened. Special Forces soldiers must be able to act on their own and as part of a team. They need to be intelligent and able to master many skills. A Special Forces soldier must also be able to parachute, make a survival camp, read maps and operate communications gear, use many kinds of weapons, and operate many machines. Special Forces in Afghanistan were even called on to ride horses on some missions.

Once an applicant makes it into one of the training programs that each Special Force unit runs, the real work begins. For some, the training will be the hardest thing they have ever done…or will ever do.

Text-Dependent Questions

1. What year were the Navy SEALs established?
2. What war ended in 1945?
3. Name three U.S. Special Forces units.

Research Project

Look up information about the founding of Special Forces outside the United States. What missions were some of them were used for? How do their operations differ from U.S. Special Forces?

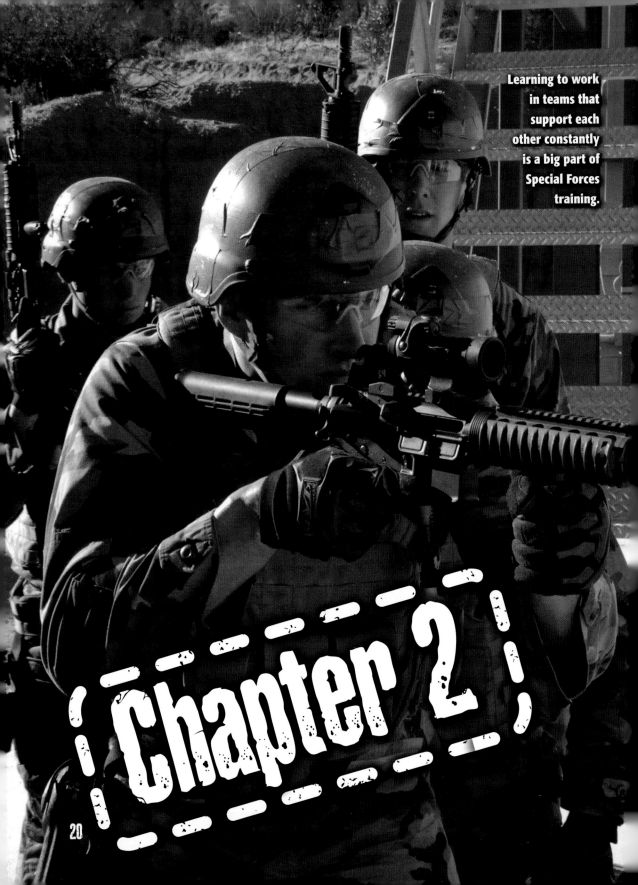

Learning to work in teams that support each other constantly is a big part of Special Forces training.

Chapter 2

Training Mind and Body

Every Special Forces unit demands the best. Becoming a full member calls for a period of intense physical training and classroom work. Because every member of every team has to be the best of the best, the process for choosing those teams is grueling. Each unit has its own way of selecting its members. Those methods include weeks of hard work, weapons training, live-fire exercises, and more. The training is designed to weed out anyone who would not be able to complete the missions. For just about every Special Forces unit, the number of people who start the process is much higher than the number who finish.

Words to Understand

hydrographic of or relating to characteristic features of bodies of water

probationary subjection of an individual to a period of testing and trial to ascertain job fitness

rappelling descending a rock face or other near-vertical surface by using a doubled rope coiled around the body and fixed at a higher point

reconnaissance military observation of a region to locate an enemy or ascertain strategic features

21

As of 2015, Special Forces in the United States were only open to male soldiers. Female soldiers have worked alongside Special Forces on missions in Iraq and Afghanistan, but their roles were not combat-oriented. There is debate among some people about letting women into Special Forces, but that has not happened yet.

After passing initial tests for the Special Forces, soldiers are sent to training camps. One of the most well known is the camp run by the Navy SEALs. Here's an in-depth run down of their process. Most Special Forces run similar camps.

Fitness First

Start with eyesight. Future Navy Seals must have nearly perfect vision, though in some cases they can wear eyeglasses to correct their vision. They have to be high school graduates and pass a physical exam. They take standardized Army tests and must reach a set level of high scores on those.

To be part of these elite units, you must be able to withstand heat, navigate water, and have the stamina of an Olympic athlete. The military does not expect recruits to start in perfect condition, but they must be in excellent shape. Each force has its own starting points, but this list from the Navy SEAL training plan might give you an idea of how fit a potential team member should be... to start. The "rest period" on the list is the time allowed between each task. In other words, you have to do all these things within about an hour.

Test	Time Limit	Rest Period
500-yard swim using breast- and/or side-stroke	12.5 minutes	10 minutes
Perform a minimum of 42 push-ups	2 minutes	2 minutes
Perform a minimum of 50 sit-ups	2 minutes	2 minutes
Perform a minimum of 6 pull-ups	No time limit	10 minutes
Run 1.5 miles wearing boots and long pants	11.5 minutes	

If you pass these qualifications, you qualify to be part of the BUD/S Physical Screen Test. BUD/S is an acronym for Basic Underwater Demolition/SEAL. During the first eight weeks, recruits are trained in the key areas of their jobs. They also continue to work to increase their physical fitness. In SEAL training, a minimum standard of performance is set by the teachers. Any student who fails any of the tests cannot continue. Here are a few examples of standards that must be reached after three weeks of training:

- 1-mile bay swim with fins in 50 minutes;
- 2-mile ocean swim with fins in 95 minutes;
- Obstacle course in 15 minutes;
- 4-mile timed run in 32 minutes.

Hell Week

The third week of SEAL training is called "Hell Week." Not only are the workout levels increased, but students are allowed only four hours of sleep… for the week! More than two-thirds of the students fall out of the course at this point.

Hell Week lasts for more than five days. During almost the entire time, the recruits are in motion, whether exercising or doing training. One famous drill involves groups of six men carrying a huge log through running, swimming, and obstacle course drills. They are not allowed to change their gear, so they end up covered in mud or dealing with wet sand all over themselves. They paddle boats, run, lift, and survive. The lack of sleep is a

constant struggle. The Navy Web site description of Hell Week discusses recruits falling asleep in their food. Though it's a physical effort, the real struggle is mental. The men who make it through are the ones who can make their mind convince their body to go on. As the Navy says, "Having survived that severe trial, they feel literally unstoppable—that they can do anything."

The sand-filled and waterlogged uniforms of these SEAL trainees will go unchanged throughout the five days of Hell Week.

Famous Navy SEALs

While the exploits of most Navy SEALs are not publicized, here are four SEALS who have become well-known since finishing their secret missions.

Roy Boehm

Boehm is considered the godfather of all SEALs. He began as an enlisted man before becoming a SEAL, and leading SEAL Team Two. He is credited with designing and developing the SEAL training used today.

Christopher Cassidy (right)

After ten years as a SEAL, Cassidy made the transition to becoming a NASA astronaut. During his decade-long stint, Cassidy had tours in Afghanistan and the Mediterranean.

Richard Marcinko

He served as a commander in charge of SEAL Team Six and now is a popular author, with many books, including *Leadership Secrets of the Rogue Warrior* and *Vengeance*.

Eric T. Olson

He is the only former Navy SEAL to be named the head of the U.S. Special Operations Command. During his time as a SEAL during the 1970s and 1980s, he was the commander of SEAL Team Six, which was a special counter-terrorism group.

Recruits who do survive Hell Week move on to even more physical training. They also learn more about how ships and Navy operations work, and how to conduct **hydrographic** surveys and make underwater charts.

SEAL students then take extensive dive training. They learn about two types of SCUBA (Self-Contained Underwater Breathing Apparatus) diving. They also learn special combat swimmer skills. After that comes ten weeks of land warfare training. During that phase, students learn about weapons, tactics, demolitions, and **reconnaissance**. The focus is on teaching land navigation, **rappelling**, weapons training, and small-unit tactics, and to learn about land and underwater explosives. The final four weeks of the session are at San Clemente in California, where students apply what they have learned. Additional training includes parachuting, emergency medicine, and communications.

Successful graduates are assigned to a team and have to complete a six-month **probationary**

Cross a river loaded down with a heavy pack? For a Special Forces soldier, it's another day at the office.

period. If they complete that, then they officially become Navy SEALs.

Are You Ready?

SEAL training is unique with its focus on diving and water-based tactics. Other Special Forces study similar skills, but add some that are specific to their missions.

The Army Rangers and Green Berets suggest that recruits should be able to complete a two-mile run in 12-14 minutes, along with 100 sit-ups and 100 push-ups. To prepare for their courses, recruits should carry a 50-pound (23-kg) load on their back (called "rucking") and march for 5-15 miles (8-24 km) at a fast walking pace.

For the Green Berets, potential recruits should add 75-100 pull-ups, 200-300 push-ups, and 200-300 sit-ups every other day.

Those are just to get recruits started. Once the actual training begins, things get even harder.

Text-Dependent Questions

1. Are women allowed in Special Forces units?
2. What ratio/percentage of students quit during Hell Week?
3. Name three skills that SEAL trainees learn.

Research Project

Test yourself: How much time would you need to complete the initial physical fitness list for becoming a Navy SEAL? Don't overdo it; you probably won't be able to match that standard. If you have a military career in mind, however, staying fit is the first step.

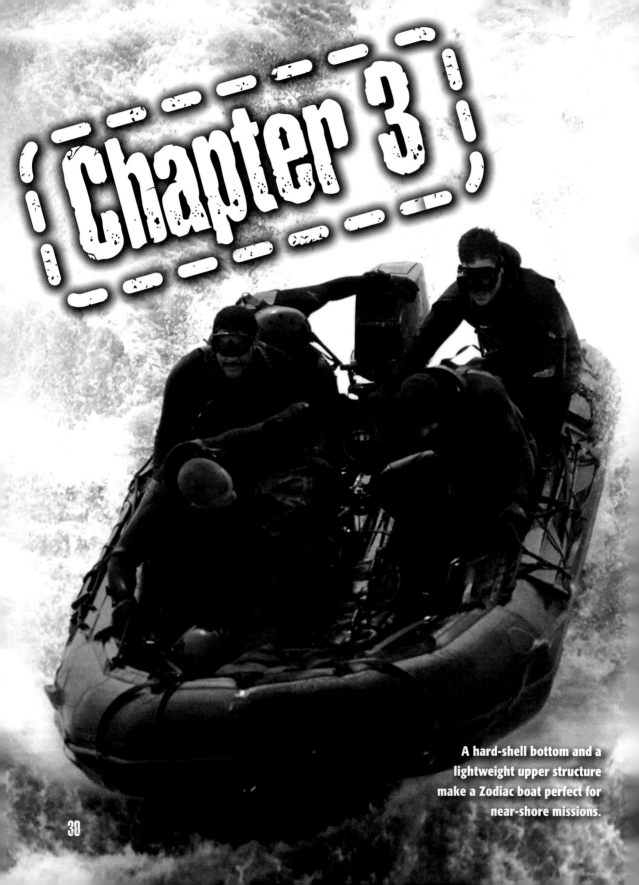

Chapter 3

A hard-shell bottom and a lightweight upper structure make a Zodiac boat perfect for near-shore missions.

Tools and Technology

Special Forces depend on their training, their teammates, and their courage when they go into the field. Along with those, however, they take with them some of the most highly advanced gear, weapons, and vehicles used by the military today. It is essential that they have the tools to do the job.

One Fast Boat

Special Forces making a landing on a beach often use an inflatable motorboat known as a Zodiac. This boat has a hard-shell bottom but air-filled sides. All military inflatable boats are designed with heavy-duty **neoprene** fabric that allows for both durability and easy repair. They are incredibly quick and easy to deploy, and can also be used as a diving platform. Though only about 15-18 feet (4.5–5.5 m) long, they can hold 1,900 to 3,700 pounds (860–1,680 kg). With a top speed of 32 mph (56 kph), they can get the soldiers to where they need to go very quickly.

Words to Understand

amplification an increase or expansion, in this case of light

fuselage the tube-shaped, main body of an aircraft

neoprene synthetic polymer resembling rubber; it is resistant to oil, heat, and weathering

Underwater Delivery

Submarines have long been used for special operations, carrying commandos, reconnaissance teams, and agents on high-risk missions. Most special operations by U.S. submarines are carried out by SEALs.

Navy SEALs can sneak to shore using this swimmer delivery system, a mini-sub that carries several soldiers.

Nuclear-powered submarines are especially well suited for this role because of their high speed, endurance, and stealth. Nuclear "boats" (all submarines are referred to as boats) make very little sound while in operation. They are also the fastest submarines in the world. By taking Special Forces operatives quietly to areas near shore, they make the missions easier to accomplish. During exercises, which include Army, Air Force, and Marine Corps special operations personnel as well as SEALs, subs pick up soldiers who parachute from fixed-wing aircraft or rappel down from helicopters into the sea. Then they travel to the mission target and send them into action.

The Navy is introducing a new sub that will be specially designed to join such operations. The New Attack Submarine will have a special chamber that will let divers leave while the sub is underwater. Plus, the sub will carry the Advanced Swimmer Delivery System (ASDS), a ten-man mini-sub for inserting and extracting Special Operations teams. Designed for short trips, the ASDS does not have crew quarters or a huge engine room or any of the other sub systems. Its small size and ease of use means that instead of swimming a mile or more underwater, Special Forces can move to within yards of a beach before leaving the craft and making their attack.

Special Forces Dogs

Not all "tools" are made of steel. Belgian Malinois dogs are trained for the Navy SEALs. The dogs attack anyone carrying a weapon and have become pivotal to special operations. The dogs can skydive from up to 25,000 feet, and work with assault team members in tunnels or rooms on missions to kill or capture the foe. They wear cameras on their heads and radio earpieces that let them communicate with their handlers.

Vision Aids

The ability to see in the dark makes operating at night possible. Special Forces wear special goggles that turn nighttime into a green-tinged form of light. The main model they use is called the AN/PVS-7. Similar models are even for sale to nonmilitary consumers.

The goggles are designed to be worn comfortably for a long time. They also can be held in the hand or mounted on a helmet. The lenses of the goggles are made to provide light **amplification** and image quality. A soldier using these cannot see colors as in the daytime, and the vision is not 100 percent as good as normal, but being able to see people move can be a huge tactical advantage. In a job that relies on secrecy and stealth, this can be the difference between success and failure.

A few years ago, the U.S. Army introduced Helmet Electronics and Display System-Upgradeable Protection—better known as HEaDS-UP. It may look like battle gear for video games, but the helmet goes way beyond fictional warfare. The HEaDS-UP system, which was developed by eyewear company Revision, includes a standard Army helmet that protects the head, neck, and face. The really cool addition is a visor on which can be projected battlefield maps, targets, health monitors, and communications, to name a few possibilities. The soldier can see everything in front of him out in the world, but he is also looking at an up-close monitor that can give him vital information. He can keep moving, watch for trouble, and still get the news and alerts he needs to complete his mission.

Nett Warrior

Away from combat, a soldier probably carries a smartphone that can give him or her all kinds of information. During battle, however, a smartphone probably would not last very long. In addition, soldiers need both hands to handle their weapons and other gear. In 2011, the Army created a way to combine the power of

One eye on the target, and one eye aided by the NETT Warrior: This soldier shows how the high-tech gear is part of the Special Forces uniform.

These Army Rangers can now use the rugged smartphones installed in chest pouches to communicate and get intelligence.

such communications devices with the mission of a Special Forces soldier.

The Nett Warrior is a battery-powered communications device that includes a monocle (like eyeglasses but with just one lens) attached to the helmet. Like the larger HEaDS-UP display, the Nett Warrior's lens shows information to the soldier, sent to him through the communications pack. In 2014, the Army added Samsung Galaxy phones to each system so that the soldiers can also receive and use live-feed video. The phones were made with a much sturdier case to help them survive the rigors of the field. The idea of the Nett Warrior is that group commanders can be in constant touch with their units and with their bases. Knowing where everyone is at all times helps keep units together. It also helps prevent tragic accidents that can happen when friendly forces fire on each other in the confusion or darkness of a battle. A radio that is part of the system has several channels to allow leaders to speak with all the people they need.

With Nett Warrior, soldiers are able to see their location, the location of their fellow soldiers, and the location of known enemies on a moving digital map.

"What this system will mean is they are never lost, never out of reach of their buddies," said Colonel Will Riggins, program manager for Soldier Warrior. "They are able to adapt to dynamics of changing combat, and able to share all that information about all aspects of their mission in order to cut through that fog of war."

The program is named after Colonel Robert Nett, who died in 2008. After joining the Army in 1940, he served until 1978. He was awarded the Medal of Honor for actions during World War II, while serving in the Philippines.

Black Hawk Helicopter

First created in 1974, the Black Hawk helicopter originated from the military's request for a transport vehicle that could fit within a C-130 Hercules. C-130s are huge cargo planes that can travel great distances. An attack helicopter usually has a smaller range, so being able to carry it inside a larger plane was a great improvement.

The Black Hawk has a 50-foot (15-m) **fuselage** length, can climb 3,000 feet (914 m) per minute, travel as fast as 195 miles (314 km) per hour, and can fly up to 19,000 feet (5,792 m) in the air. The design uses numerous structural features that allow the aircraft to remain airborne even if it suffers extreme damage. It helps protect all on board in a crash or while receiving enemy fire. It includes a strong cabin box, durable wheels that can sustain a very hard bump on land-

A pair of Black Hawks leave the runway, packed with soldiers on a mission.

ing, armor plating on the outside, and rotor blades that can withstand direct hits by bullets up to an inch (23mm) long in size.

Special Forces Weapons

To accomplish their missions, Special Forces soldiers must be heavily armed to defend themselves and others, or to attack enemy forces. Special Forces around the world choose from a wide array of small, lightweight—but deadly—armaments.

FN SCAR CQC: This assault rifle can be fitted with the FN40 grenade launcher for additional firepower. It can be fired with either hand and has tremendous accuracy. Also, a Special Forces soldier can quickly replace the standard short barrel with a longer, 16-inch (40-cm) one if the mission requires engagement at greater distances.

HK MP5N: This weapon can be fired one shot at a time or in full automatic mode. It was developed specially for use by Navy SEALs.

HK MK 23 SOCOM .45: This handgun was also created just for use by Special Forces. The U.S. Special Operations Command wanted a gun that was powerful, durable, and reliable. Because Special Forces operate in just about every environment, their weapons have to be able to deal with water, dirt, sand, cold, heat, and more.

SIG Sauer P226: This is a pistol used by Special Forces, as well as by many law enforcement agencies. It is considered one of the best in the world, and is the official sidearm of the SEALs. The weapons they use actually have an anchor engraved on the side.

AK-47: This is another assault rifle, first developed in the Soviet Union. It is one of the most reliable weapons ever made and makes for a great choice when having to swim with a weapon to the beach. It is also easy to take apart and clean in the field, with very few parts, which makes it almost impossible to jam.

From communications gear to transportation to weapons, Special Forces demand the best. Every piece of gear they carry and use might mean the difference between a successful mission…or not coming home at all.

Text-Dependent Questions

1. Why was the Black Hawk helicopter created?
2. Name the small, fast-attack boat that Special Forces often use.
3. What color does night-vision technology turn the world?

Research Project

Go online and read about heads-up displays. How are they used by other types of soldiers? Can you think of other professions where such a technology would be useful? Design what you'd like to see inside your own heads-up display.

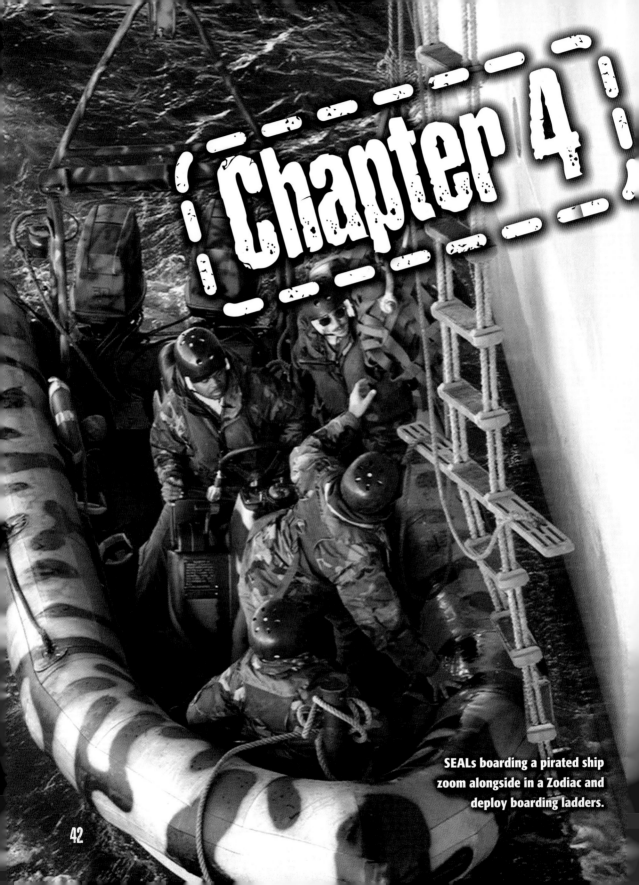

Chapter 4

SEALs boarding a pirated ship zoom alongside in a Zodiac and deploy boarding ladders.

Mission Accomplished!

The USS *Bainbridge* had arrived off the Somalia coast near the motorized lifeboat that contained four Somali pirates and American ship captain Richard Phillips.

Bainbridge Commander Frank Castellano had called in the Navy SEALs. To get them assigned to the job, the Navy had to get permission from the U.S. president, the commander-in-chief. He does not approve every single Special Forces mission, but for this one in international waters, he had to say yes. He did, and SEAL Team Six was deployed. When called, that group of SEALs was more than 8,000 miles (12,875 km) away, on the east coast of the United States.

While the *Bainbridge* crew and other American vessels surrounded the Somali pirates and Phillips, the SEALs flew from Virginia to the coast of Somalia. It was a 16-hour, nonstop journey. The plane was refueled multiple times while in the air.

Words to Understand

brandished waved or shook a weapon

negotiations discussions aimed at reaching an agreement

The team parachuted into the ocean in the middle of the night, hidden from the pirates. They climbed aboard the small vessel USS *Halyburton* in the early morning hours. They were then sent to the USS *Bainbridge*.

Armed with sniper rifles, the SEALs were flat on the deck of *Bainbridge* with their sights set on the lifeboat. Then it was just a matter of waiting for the right moment to strike.

Later that same day, as the weather worsened, the pirates agreed to be towed out further into the ocean by the *Bainbridge*. That placed the lifeboats out of the worst waves while allowing time for more **negotiations**. The *Bainbridge* narrowed the distance between it and the lifeboat to within 25 yards (22.8 m).

The next morning, the youngest Somali pirate, just 16 years old, asked to come aboard the *Bainbridge*. He gave himself up so he could receive medical aid to the hand he injured during the attack on the *Maersk Alabama* four days earlier. That left just three pirates on the lifeboat.

A little while later, when one of the pirates **brandished** his rifle as he approached Phillips from behind, the SEAL Team Six sharpshooters fired. Each of the three pirates was killed with a single shot. The SEALs quickly swarmed over the lifeboat to make sure there were no more pirates. Phillips was safe; mission accomplished.

Captain Phillips was free, ending the first pirate hijacking of a United States vessel since the early 1800s, when Thomas Jefferson was president.

If not for the parachuting ability and sharp-shooting skills of a Navy SEALs platoon, the outcome could have been vastly different. It was another successful outcome for an elite team of Special Forces.

Quick action by a SEAL team led to this happy meeting between USS *Bainbridge* Commander Frank Castellano (left) and hostage Captain Richard Phillips.

Find Out More

Books

Inside Special Forces (Ten-book series). New York: Rosen Publishing, 2015.

Military Jobs (Five-book series). New York: Cavendish Square, 2015.

Whiting, Jim. *U.S. Special Forces: Delta Force.* Mankato, Minn.: Creative Paperbacks, 2015. Note: The author has several other books on specific Special Force units.

Web Sites

www.navyseals.com/nsw/navy-seal-history/
Official history of the Navy Seals.

http://www.specialforcesassociation.org/about/sf-history/
History of several Special Forces.

www.military.com/military-fitness/army-special-operations/army-green-beret-training
Find out how to get ready to be a Green Beret.

Series Glossary of Key Terms

apprehending capturing and arresting someone who has committed a crime

assassinate kill somebody, especially a political figure

assessment the act of gathering information and making a decision about a particular topic

contraband material that is illegal to possess

cryptography another word for writing in code

deployed put to use, usually in a military or law-enforcement operation

dispatcher a person who announces emergencies over police radio and helps organize the efforts of first responders

elite among the very best; part of a select group of successful experts

evacuated moved to a safe location, away from danger

federal related to the government of the United States, as opposed to the government of an individual state or city

forensic having to do with crime scene evidence

instinctive based on natural impulse and done without instruction

interrogate to question a person as part of an official investigation

Kevlar an extra-tough fabric used in bulletproof vests

search-and-rescue the work of finding survivors after a disaster occurs, or the team that does this work

stabilize make steady or secure; also, in medicine, make a person safe to transport

surveillance the act of watching another person or a place, usually from a hidden location

trauma any physical injury to the body, usually involving bleeding

visa travel permit issued by a government to a citizen for a specific trip

warrant official document that allows the police to do something, such as arrest a person

Index

Photo Credits

About the Author

Matthew Marini was an editor with NFL Publishing and has contributed to numerous national publications. He also is the project manager for the National Football League's *Record & Fact Book*, an annual publication that offers historical and new information on all 32 NFL teams and the Pro Football Hall of Fame, as well as an extensive records section. Marini lives in California.